The Past Is
a
Dangerous Driver

poems

Neal Mason

Holland Park Press London

Published by Holland Park Press 2022
Copyright © Neal Mason 2022

First Edition

The moral right of Neal Mason to be identified as the
author of this work has been asserted by hin in accordance
with the Copyright, Designs and Patents Act of 1988.

British Library Cataloguing-in-Publication Data
A catalogue record for this book is available from the British Library

ISBN 978-1-907320-95-8

Cover designed by Reactive Graphics

Printed and bound by
CPI Group (UK) Ltd, Croydon CR0 4YY

www.hollandparkpress.co.uk

To R.H.

CONTENTS

After Dunwich   11
Derelict Classroom   13
The Long Campaign   15
7th December   19
Holiday Romance   21
Martello Tower   22
Wooden Ruler   24
Mendel, Shopping   25
Affinity   28
Reflected on Water   30
SS Saxon Star   39
The Figure   40
Not as a Medal   43
Slowing Down   44
World War II Bomb   46
Lineage   48
Journal of a Tree   54
The Stratagem   56
Breakages   63
Submersion   65
The Grand Nitrator   67
The Museum of Lost Art   69
The Pied Piper   71
SPQR   72
Contiguity   74

Acknowledgements   81

AFTER DUNWICH

Poised mid stride, the sea hesitates
like a convert with doubts.
On the crumbling shore, the church waits
for deepest night, new moon
repairing a trefoil. Seeming to decide,
footsteps that slap on the porch
belong to the spring tide.

In the graveyard, waves that were grass
are real water;
crosses, each a spar and mast
heading east, sink like ships,
the wind tolling passing-bells,
sea water running for sanctuary
as the congregation swells

and pushes back doors. A slow procession
fills the nave
to overflowing, takes possession
of each aisle as it gradually advances
to ankle depth, or hems of cassocks,
small waves bowing
low, kneeling on hassocks.

Transepts flood, become black bays
in whose waters
the trefoil moon bobs and sways,
choir screen a permeable wall,
its pattern shrinking ever shorter.
Half a nave away
the font is filling with water.

Bubbles rise in streams, twirling and clowning
from buried vaults
as though each occupant were drowning.
The lectern, an eagle clutching darkness,
becomes a seabird, glares at the procession
rising higher and higher
and teaching its own lesson.

Foam mounts the pulpit steps,
seems to sigh
a sermon drawn from hidden depths.
The equinoctial gale outside
intones and chants, presses and batters
the church's beleaguered hull;
an oriel window, like a porthole, shatters.

The bulkhead of the altar cannot halt
the will of the tide;
old wounds sting with new salt
as a figure seems to cling
to wreckage. The absent choir's refrain
seems to wail from the heavens, its descant
lashing, secular rain.

As the waves advance, all in their grip,
the kingdom succumbs,
appears to invert. Its floundering ship,
roof a hull, beams awash,
drifts in the sea where it articles toss,
lightning conducted down
no intercessory cross.

DERELICT CLASSROOM

Foxgloves face the windows, vacantly
gaze out, but learn nothing
from chattering thrushes and blackbirds
or the sky blank as doubt;
knowledge and order are lost in overgrowth
and Nature's grown up a lout.

What were pellets flicked in fun
are flies. Lazy chalk dust
used to drift like pollen,
motes in young eyes,
where now the beams of a blinding sun
glare in rank surprise.

The walls are covered in graffiti, the vandal
moss. The green blackboard
fails to instruct brambles
which increase, oblivious of loss,
while a snail's trail, looping and curling
beneath, serves for a gloss.

Where the red roof was is white and blue
sky; clouds, unformed
and uninformed of nimbus
or cumulus, writhe as they try
outlines a teacher might approve
and on which textbooks can rely.

A puffball is the globe that children held
in awe, its national colours
now brown, not the variety
primary childhood saw;
the spores would mature to khaki, then fall,
obeying some natural law.

Beyond the broken glass grow pampas
and canes; wind-punished nettles
sting empty air
while butterflies play games
on buddleia. The wilderness encroaches, unaware
of culture, geography or names.

THE LONG CAMPAIGN

In York minster's undercroft, remains
of the 9th Legion's principia, I listen
for the march of feet, whisper
a roll call.

Are you there?
Were you ever?
Six thousand names
withhold an answer. Did you march
out of Eboracum and history
to disappear in some secret slaughter?
Dessert? Or simply exist
in the quartermaster's mind?

Too wily, or too old,
to fall for such tactics, I return
to the command vehicle, throw away
maps, SAM codes, Queen's Regulations
and refer, not to Standing Orders,
but to standing stones,
tumuli, river crossings,
the stars. Which way
has the Ninth gone? Where
will the ambush be?

On Wheeldale Moor
the Roman road directs us
to mist and sky and solitude.
Cautiously, we advance, gain ground
through clumps of heather, *Calluna vulgaris*,
field glasses magnifying
danger, grouse alarmed
by footsteps, or thunder, or the need
to be alarmed. The Light Infantry,
Aucto Splendore Resurgo, reconnoitres
and reports it has found
mist and sky and solitude.

Where are they, these soldiers
who've hidden their amphitheatre
from us? They play games, their presence
in York doubtful, as though suggestion
could be made of stone. Their ghosts
of forts observe us, broken crags
reinforced by cloud.

Fog descends
and the world dissolves to stone
grey. The A169 seems to cobble
beneath our feet, tank tracks cracking
the surface of things. Then,
through a gap in the mist, we glimpse them
lined up on a limestone ridge.

In battle formation, we wait
for ages and the sun's dispensation. Its rays
back them, silhouettes with sharp
glinting edges whose substance
gave names to what we do. I despatch
envoys, attempt to come to terms
with the past, but old campaigners know
progress, or process, means
confrontation. My messengers
fail to return.

Entrenched, a Lance Corporal
sights a legionary's shape, an oblong,
so he aims at a scintilla of light,
the shield's boss, and waits. The day
manoeuvres itself, midday positions
unassailable, time in deadlock. An Emperor
moth, *Saturnia pavonia*, parades nearby,
then is gone.

A shower of pilums
buckles on impact. The Lance Corporal
stumbles, pulls the trigger. A gap
exposes sunlight as a shadow falls,
quickly filled by another. Curlews sheer off
as attacks are countered, swords flashing
like gunfire. Roman standards
defy insignia, a modern regiment
pinned down by the past.

I call in planes. They strafe
moorland, limestone, peat, soften up
a churned landscape
history won't notice. Tank tracks,
as though on Roman roads, point
straight at the hilltop, armour rocking
and nodding as though in agreement. Shells
burst, eardrums defended by hands
as a bugle, or *cornu*, orders discord.
The Lance Corporal, identity tags
indestructible, sinks down, becomes
a shadow in a fold of hills.

The battle turns
into a war of attrition
and I'm sure
Christmas will be over before it.
In the Minster, requiems echo
round classical architecture,
never quite fade, and we may as well
read Tacitus for news of the front.
Gradually, we advance, we're assured,
in a just cause, sure of our ground,
convinced we can never settle
for the status quo.

7TH DECEMBER
'A date that will live in infamy'

As though it was my fault.
A Sunday too – not that the Japs
cared about a Christian day of rest.
Infamous? You forget
I gave birth to Bernini, Mascagni,
Mary Queen of Scots – well,
you can't win them all.

I'm the feast of St. Ambrose
(who the hell was he?). I saw off
Hobbema, hanged Robert Kett,
executed Marshal Ney.
Perhaps you're right;
I'm a bit of a swine, aren't I?

Yesterday swells at giving birth
to Joseph Conrad. Tomorrow boasts
of Horace, Sibelius and the first
English actress on the stage (he can't
remember her name). As for the 5th
that drunkard repealed prohibition.
To sober him up, I remind him
he opened Preston by-pass.

I dawned peacefully enough.
It's not as though I was howling
gales, murdering fishermen, battering
seabirds against rocks. I just
yawned. It can be boring
being December 7th. But I woke up
when carriers and Zeros appeared
on my horizon. As the noise began
(I still had a hangover
from the 5th) I looked longingly
at the International Date Line.

If, for a dirty weekend, you chose
Hawaii and me, maybe you feel
peeved. But what you do with me
and each other is your affair.
Time for bed.

Have a nice day.

HOLIDAY ROMANCE

Since we sunbathed on this shore
a year ago, waves have ushered Crete
two inches south, which leaves me
two thousand miles distant,
plus two inches more,
from your eyes, your arms, your mouth.

What to you was just a vacation
was a lifetime to me; weeks of living
love's mythology. But you
talked science, crusty tectonics,
instead of a deeper formation,
so we differed in more than chronology.

If I lie here for a thousand years,
as it seems I have, or until the grains of sand
are ground to dust, or Greece
and Turkey touch and peacefully unite,
the kissing of waves in my ears
will be a gentle echo of us.

MARTELLO TOWER

On a stormy night
we lie in bed
and listen to the past invade.
The advance guard, Napoleon's
can opener, howls up the beach, spray
lashing like musket balls,
crashing waves a cannonade.
Six-foot-thick walls tremble
as our revolving gun fires,
a cannonball moon, sulphurous
in smoky cloud, flashing
through windows.
If we had a corner
our dog would cower in it. Instead
of ammunition, our curved cupboards
store baguettes, Ardennes pate,
Camembert among towering
cans of beans, the wine rack's
gun barrels pointing from Burgundy,
Cotes du Rhone, Medoc
and all the sleepy regions
whose soldiers attack tonight.
Around our bookshelves, history leans
on fiction, Paine on Hardy,
Rousseau on Rousseau,
a bust of Wellington defiant
on a French-polished table.

Towards morning
the storm subsides, but the rumbling
persists; deep below us
troops of tourists invade
through the Tunnel, casualties – words,
laws, weights and measures – mounting
as Brussels, near Waterloo,
advances its armies again.

WOODEN RULER

With this flat stick I ruled my world
of strange shapes and angles
unknown to geometry, lines wavering,
too thick, page corners curled,
my mind, like Nature, rarely straight,
but crenellated, circuitous, whorled.

My straight-line graphs, corrugated like iron,
seemed to chart unease,
schoolmates all strangers,
good for a laugh, but not to rely on;
among the staff were women, but no
curved shoulder to cry on.

I began to explore the grounds, learn the angles,
get the measure of my world,
the Head's cane, the bent teachers
breaking bounds. Memory rambles
constantly round the school fields,
snags on looping brambles.

Now I'll type these lines and end the page,
ruling it off freehand.
Shapes and forms appeal, but not
strict confines, latent rage
exploring and testing, though wary of leaving
the bounds of an earlier age.

MENDEL, SHOPPING

Tins of processed peas,
as though evolved
from Warhol's primal soup,
line the shelves, proclaim
the sweetness of selection.
Repetitious
pop music, foodstuff
of fame, lives its fifteen minutes
again. While lighting
strips each shadow
to the bone, Mendel picks
the peas, alone.

Conspicuous, his habit,
evolved as uniform,
seems singular among jeans'
mass-individuality.
Supermarket children's
repetitious
jibes, their tee-shirts'
banality, only remind him
of finality, the lack
of expressive faces,
half grown, troublesome perhaps,
but like his own.

Weighing, in his hand,
a tin, its sameness
guaranteed, he calculates
the probabilities of choice,
consistency a benefit,
repetitious,
for which multitudes of shoppers
rejoice as though one, and in one
voice. Mathematically
he seems at home, Austria
far away, but thoroughness
was different in his day.

Reading the bar-code
as though genetic,
he wonders whether taste
is as uniform as price.
But inflation, imperceptible,
repetitious,
mutates, constructs its own
device, levels every palate
to entice greater custom.
The labels are colourful, attractively
displayed; Mendel ponders
heredity's dubious trade.

After so much choice,
as though his own,
the checkout looms. A divine
girl, who's bored but smiles,
makes the best of a bad job,
repetitious;
for a moment it's not Augustine
who beguiles, his order rewarded
with trials and tribulations,
but a might-have-been
content, a life
enjoyed, not spent.

Mendel turns and leaves
the produce of the time,
its repetitious
rows of laden shelves
like those his work, unread,
will lie on when he's dead.
His humble, hybrid peas
fed and nourished
creative minds that bred
leaps in thought; mental
athletics whose mutant offspring
bear the label 'Genetics'.

Affinity

New school cold as a Finnish winter,
he lies in bed crying. Unaware
of all but dissonance and fear, he can't know
that, many miles from here,
Sibelius lies dying.

Is this, then, home? Wandering the grounds,
he's a solitary, shivering waif. How can he find
his way through boyhood's estate, or tell that maturity
will be like the fruitless wait
for Sibelius's Eighth?

Geography: Growing Finland has lost its Mother
Russia, fends for itself. His own republic,
he finds his own course, embraces the woods
that provide his only resource
and source of wealth.

History: Sweden and Russia raged and tugged
like parents whose love is aggression. Finland, benighted,
joined with Fascists to fight, not for darkness,
but a glimpse of summer sunlight
in winter's possession.

Mathematics: Amidst the season's bleak
remainders – his greatest friends – white geometry
connects what tries to grow, nothing subtracting
from the multiple oneness of snow.
The fraction mends.

He listens to legends in leaves, tone poems
bowed by boughs of trees. A long way south
of Sibelius's music was home, but he warmed
to winter and made it his own;
a permanent freeze.

A blank page waits in the school exam,
his best subject nail-biting, no theme
entering his head; but then, suddenly composed,
his hand conducting a pen,
he begins writing.

REFLECTED ON WATER

1

I began in a scull at Henley
as though in a race,
but where I was going, between beech woods
and meadows, and at such a pace,
I had little idea, but the obstacle, doubt,
couldn't stop me, nor the locks, nor Hambleden Weir.

At Marlow I overtook Shelley
with Mary in tow;
over-laden with theories and books, straight down
was the only way he could go.
A storm is brewing, as though for practice,
and Shelley's vision starts slipping and slewing.

Drifting leisurely, I observe,
like a reporter,
Stanley Spencer pouring troubled oils
on Cookham's placid water;
Christ is news and preaches while walking
past fishermen's floats and coxless crews.

Rowing choppily in the wake
of three men in a boat,
I rescue their dog, which successfully yaps
and splutters, but neglects to float;
supporting its chin, I consider mouth-
to-mouth, hesitate, then throw it back in.

Sunlight on water and willow
is always at play, Sir,
a constant panorama, yet forever changing,
for this is the village of Bray, Sir,
a few coats a season, always adapting
for tourists, survival the perennial reason.

I pull strongly towards Windsor's
jig-saw walls,
a thousand-year picture whose every piece
puzzles; incompleteness enthrals,
like the Guildhall by Wren, its columns short
of the ceiling – though not of the floor. Ahem.

On the cerebral side of the river
lies battered Eton.
Flogged black and blue, let Gladstone stand
(he can't sit) for all who were beaten,
which must exclude the Duke of Wellington,
though Britain v. Europe is an unresolved feud.

But now in my scull I stand
precariously to attention.
I face north and salute with my pen hand
Stoke Poges, my intention
to honour a grave. Boat rocking,
perhaps he replies with a friendly wave.

I arrive at Hampton Court Palace
behind Wolsey's barge.
Looking ahead, I see William III
deciding which bits to enlarge,
embellishing, designing, his and Mary's
hundreds of rooms apparently confining.

I pass by the glories of Hampton
for concrete and glass.
I welcome Kingston's housing estates,
factories and private grass
and fly on wings to a single stone
'functional' at the crowning of Saxon kings.

One's alabaster breast shivers
on Strawberry Hill
where Walpole's gothic Castle of Otranto
gives architects the horrors still,
though today it's enlightening; it's a college for teachers –
but they, to many, are more frightening.

I rush to buy a ticket at Twickenham
as though in a scrum,
press forward, tackle the crowds,
then stop, suddenly numb.
I lose hope; they're thronging to see
rugby, not the grounds of the matchless Pope.

Curious, I look for Isleworth,
the place I was born,
and see a child waving from the bank,
his familiar expression forlorn
as a gale at Kew. I call encouragement
for his future journey. Enjoy the view.

Near Hogarth's house is a kid
etched by the road,
unwashed by its single parent.
(Marriage is not a la mode,
nor is grace; politeness progressed
with its elbows when denim superseded lace.)

The Oxford and Cambridge crews
of a hundred years
race to Putney. I consider stopping
at Young's brewery for a couple of beers
(there's an extra stress, so maybe more).
London decides with a potent YES.

2

While the vague sky is scratched
by precise jets,
I gaze doubtfully at my map of the Thames,
consider the course of my quest.
Anchorless, I sway, a bobbing craft
that might be going the wrong way.

The National Army Museum,
with its guns and swords,
neighbours Chelsea Flower Show.
Such incongruity rewards
the searching mind; reflect on the River
and a muddy cloud may be all you find.

I scull past barges of sightseers
at Westminster Pier.
I see, storming Westminster Bridge,
a charioted Boadicea,
the traffic scattering. Parliament, of course,
doesn't notice and carries on nattering.

The Thames seems frozen at Southwark,
a polar waste
as Scott's 'Discovery' clears me a path,
my personal Antarctic replaced
by a terror as blank; I shiver to glimpse
the desolate frigidity of the South Bank.

Then I'm lost in a mist
Monet is painting.
His brushes dab and sweep all round me,
but now somebody's tainting
his chimney stacks, his beautiful smog;
the inartistic Clean Air Acts.

It's summer again as I spot
the dome of St. Paul's.
The Whispering Gallery echoes the name
of the genius who designed these walls –
but my voice screams, 'WHICH CONCRETE BLOCKHEAD
BUILT OFFICES AND TOWERS AS SCREENS?'

Something nudges my memory
at the College of Arms;
it hints that heredity is more permanent
than a journey's fleeting charms,
so I keep moving. My brain may be weak,
but my thighs and biceps are certainly improving.

It's a load of bollocks that Billingsgate
is a byword for swearing,
that the prats who sell sprats are twats in flat hats
their foulmouthed fishwives aren't wearing,
so no more quips. I stop
to stuff my mouth with a codpiece and chips.

Silent as a ghost I slide
past Traitors' Gate.
Although I row against the tide,
I'm facing myself, an innate
need to go back. For me, ferries,
coaches and trains are on the wrong track.

The Conqueror's White Tower
lays a shadow of grey.
I hear the fading cries and sighs
of a language locked away.
The ravens call; if they desert
and songbirds sing, the Tower will fall.

The arms of Tower Bridge
exult for me.
Captured cannon from Waterloo
salute those newly free
of the walled city. At the Mayflower pub
I'm a sober pilgrim (more's the pity).

Trying to escape from Stepney
(and who can blame him?)
Judge Jeffries hides from his life
and times, but history will name him
when it revises. His whole life
in two words: Bloody Assizes.

Like the pride of the British Navy,
my scull a cruiser,
I arrive at Greenwich and zero longitude,
though I'm no sextant-user.
The Observatory's observed, a maritime power's
grave, the hulks of its buildings preserved.

Many fathoms below me
people in bubbles
are sucked through the straw of Blackwall Tunnel.
My striking-rate doubles
at East India docks. I leave the Thames
for the River Lea, history as cox.

3

I began in a scull, though Henley
could have been anyplace,
and the way I was going, facing backwards
while rushing ahead, was a race
through challenging water, but the odds on succeeding,
or at least not failing, are growing shorter.

I splash through Hackney Marshes
triangled with sails.
The largest council estate in the world
is Dagenham to the east, not Wales
as I'd naturally thought. I now sense my goal;
its tiny pier will seem like a port.

Alexandra Palace drew pictures
I don't want to see;
if culture's become quiz games and soaps,
sit-coms and the National Lottery,
give me savages; word-hoard and rhythm,
at least, were enhanced by Beowulf's ravages.

I'm closer to my quarry at Chingford
where good Queen Bess
has a quiet hunting lodge, timber framed,
not designed to impress,
therefore impressive. She wonders why
modern 'statements' seem retrogressive.

At Gentlemen's Row in Enfield
I chat to Lamb,
Mary, his younger sister, referred to
as delicately as one can,
politeness for cover; we talk of journeys
and avoid mention of their stabbed Mother.

Epping Forest is a blaze
of golden leaves.
I fly like an arrow glancing off trees
and rocks as the water weaves
back and forth. My target is close;
it watches and waits a mile to the north.

Today, like the motorway
speeding nearby,
is a concrete illusion, a constant diversion
the spirit tries to defy.
For the survivor, unassimilated,
powerful, the past is a dangerous driver.

At last it pulls into view,
my journey's end.
I'm not here for the Norman nave
or the tower, but an old friend
and a lost era. Within me survives
the loyalty and affinity which drew us nearer.

That Tennyson lived nearby
half slips my mind.
In memoriam Harold Godwinson
I wander the ruins and find
history shabby, so reconstruct
the grounds and original Waltham Abbey.

Come into the garden,
overgrown.
Summer's gone, flowers picked
and I'm standing here all alone.
A heady scent. My first time here,
yet this was a place I used to frequent.

I've found where I need to be
and burned my boat.
There's no going back on going back
to a history not remote
but all around. Though waves of change
have threatened, engulfed and drowned
much of note and the effort seems great
and the scenery strange,
I continue to float.

SS SAXON STAR
December 1946

'Omelette, Sir?' The Captain's table
groans. A peacetime sea boils
round our saucepan of a ship,
storms threatening its cargo
of forty-six million eggs.
Perhaps all stewards are jesters.
Canada behind us, Gulf Stream
warming our hull, he served
poached eggs. Britons are hungry
for comedians, so, when we dock,
Merseysiders will be delighted
he's returning to Canada. Jokes about
eggs should be rationed. But
they can't know his Father and brothers
served in the merchant marine,
sailed with Atlantic convoys
in a single ship; that torpedoes,
like sperms after an egg,
sought their ship and found it
laden with oil. They were fried.
So I laugh heartily at his quips
and eat what I'm given.

THE FIGURE

At the still point of dawn
when shadows stretch
and seem to yawn and the mist
curls, late to rise,
yesterday retreats to a dark wood,
mingles quietly with shade and leaves,
then waits, but in disguise.

For the girl, happy in her school
where boisterousness
and laughter rule, sadness
is merely a florid graze.
Pain and sorrow adopt the colours
left behind by a livid dusk,
quickly yesterday's.

The new day has won,
night compacted
by a westering sun which burns,
leaflike, the past away.
Then out of the wood walks a figure,
slow, old, its face veined
as foliage, but grey.

For the woman sitting alone,
her relinquished child
quarter grown, the years
since she let her go
adopt a dark and hollow tone,
her younger, overheated love
a repressed glow.

The grey figure comes.
Though pale and old,
it un-numbs resolve
never really cool,
so that, like a ghost, she begins
to walk, to wander ever nearer
her daughter's colouring-book school.

The illuminated wood,
divested by light
of its canopy, or hood, suggests
it could never lie.
The breeze prods, upending leaves
the sun grills, their innocence
expressed by a sigh.

In the playground, surrounded
by a fence, the girl
stops, dumbfounded; a woman
weeps and calls her name.
Through the mesh, the woman begs
love and forgiveness, pleads tearfully
she wasn't to blame.

All restraint gone,
she beats the ground
she falls upon, screams
the girl belongs to her.
Teachers rush, quick to protect
a child who sees too clearly
through eyes that blur.

As the years stretch her form,
her mind compacts
that revealing dawn like leaves
where her Mother lies interred.
Growing, she learns to forget, except
when night-time suggests nothing's lost,
merely deferred.

The wood, each season,
lives and dies
for no other reason than cloud,
sunshine, wind and rain.
Whatever was, in branch or leaf,
in fruit or flower or twisted trunk,
will be again.

And the girl has met a man
who forgets his marriage,
as passion can, but returns
later to his wife for good.
The girl, pregnant, considers her choices,
decides on adoption. A grey figure
begins to emerge from the wood…

NOT AS A MEDAL

Give me metal said Beaverbrook,
Minister of Aircraft Production, so
our garden railings are somewhere
over Germany, encroach
on lebensraum, and my frying pan
chases Messerschmidts. Hanging
next to my iron, I owned
a piece of Spitfire, my colander,
no longer full of holes, I hope. But
my son is up there too, flying
pieces of bikes, prams, Epstein,
someone's best cutlery, and I pray
he returns as he was,
not as a medal.

SLOWING DOWN

Endangered, each species migrates
south across the Americas. A halting
Mustang falters, cools in the Sierra Madre
by a burnt-out Firebird. Cherokees
roam the tropics, trail, then overtake
a Cheyenne. Fins rusting, Stingrays
reflect by the Amazon's banks
while blowing Impalas bump by.
Herds of leaky convertibles
head for the sun, headlamps dim,
leather seats wrinkled with age,
bald tyres breaking the highway code,
but obeying a severer law.
The further south the older: in Rio
a thirsty Prohibition Packard
taxis the ghosts of hoodlums; one expects
to see Capone step out, or Bogart,
and sometimes does. In the Pampas, Jaguars
avoid the Pierce-Arrow. A few surviving
Model Ts, once ubiquitous as buffalo,
find their way to the Cape,
but slowly. Setting off in the First War,
they began to brake in Paraguay
ineffectually, many converted to black scrap
abruptly. Half buried
in the Patagonian Desert, a Locomobile rests
its two and a half tons and nine litre engine,
radiator boiled long ago, mammoth
silver body sinking slowly in sand.

Seven thousand miles north,
the latest shiny model, faster
than ever and with classic, ageless lines,
begins to clock up the mileage
that will lead to this pile of sand.

WORLD WAR II BOMB

Drain repairs for an excavation,
your ever-present threat
exposed; five hundred pounds
of rusting death
part of our foundations.

Your victims died
of old age. We disinter you,
dispose of your remains with respect
due to caution, not reverence,
all our retrospective ease
reconsidered. Scenes flash back
like a Pathé news: the cot rocking
a few feet above you; parties,
the house vibrating
with music; VE Day celebrations,
survivors laughing, re-living
closeness to death.

The bomb disposal squad,
grandchildren of your war, tiptoes
where we confidently strode.
A siren wails somewhere
deep inside my head;
in a private blackout, I sense
the rhythm of bombers' engines
through ack-ack and searchlights
as you fall closer.

The explosion
twists metal windows, Art Deco
fireplace in flames, alters
small histories, kills my grandparent
years before I'm born.

Someone, an air raid warden,
goes back to a gap
in the terrace.

The War recedes, but his
two-minute silence lasts
a lifetime. Wife and descendants –
ideas buried in a rubble of thought –
wander his rented room. He stares
into the fire, thinks he hears us,
his possibilities, a chattering of generations
who anticipate birthdays, anniversaries
and ask about the War. In a sideboard,
by a pile of empty photo frames,
newspaper cuttings yellow, report
battles, births, marriages,
deaths. A shoe box contains
a scarred ring, tarnished badges,
a ration book. Coming to,

I sense the all-clear, bomb
de-fused, bumping on a truck,
a quarter of a ton of alternative
history carted away to be scrapped.

LINEAGE

My Father – or a man who might
have been – drives through the night,
headlights joining the dotted line.
From a damp cottage, she watches for a sign
of the car she knows she can never share;
the cost of petrol to drive there
is more than she earns in a week. I gaze
at genealogy's dotted line, seek ways
of joining driver to cottage dweller,
uniting heir with produce-seller,
but the man has turned and slowed, hides
while I search in the dark, then rides
unseen to a fork in the road.

The cheque I sign for the Alvis – a black
saloon from the forties – is another scrap
in the paperchase. I've followed the trail
through records and false accounts, avail
myself of stories and money perhaps
not mine. I accelerate through gaps
in history's traffic to the cottage whose shell
lies in the future, where it fell.
Sunshine speeds up the bonnet and dies;
the moon leaps high and flies.
Somewhere ahead is a car, lights
on the door of the girl whose nights
history has left ajar.

I park the Alvis at the gate. Seeds
of starlight, prolific on wet weeds,
create a garden no longer decayed.
Jazz from a gramophone, softly played,
drifts from the cottage and down the path;
inside, her perfume and a fire on the hearth.
In a note, its haste, she says, due
to her condition, she provides a clue
for her lover. Reading too, I thank
the reference to 'what follows' (it's blank)
for hinting what it could be. The heir
read, and saw with despair
that 'what follows' is me.

Leaving the cottage, I return to the car
to ponder my next move. The bar
of the village inn is empty. I sink
back in a chair and try to think
where they'd meet, consider the choices.
From the lounge, a murmur of voices.
After an hour of aimless thought,
my mind wanders round the things I've bought,
the dubious deals a legacy can afford –
then, from the lounge, I catch the word 'fraud'.
Perfume fills the air. I run
to the lounge door like one
possessed. But nobody's there.

Perhaps I seek, but fear to find.
How much would I pay for peace of mind?
My Father – or the man who could
have been – began to weep as he stood
in the dock. Heir to a family firm,
he embezzled, but never served his term
in gaol. The secret legacy that's mine,
if it followed that dotted line,
is a question my own past begs;
how much is bequeathed between one's legs?
The girl in the inn had cried, baby
on the way, and her lover, maybe,
a man who cheated and lied.

The road signs are modern, the direction
the same, her hours of introspection
now minutes in the fast lane.
My Father applies for bail, in vain,
while I catch up and overtake the past.
It's my Mother's first journey – and last –
her lover far away; instead,
I park at the clinic, then sit by her bed.
The stigma in her arms wails as though
it would tell the distant village. They know.
My Mother's hand looks old, takes mine
and passes on what time
has given to her to hold.

Do I confide to an empty bed?
She hears, responding to what's said,
her 'condition' – me – tearful, crying
as I confess to a life of lying
and fraud. She seems to acknowledge, weakly,
anachronistic care, obliquely
refers to provision being made,
but not its source, nor who paid.
I stare at the baby; he stares at me,
but, instead of clear eyes, I see
guilt and fear and shame, a look
aware I knowingly forsook
the chance of redeeming our name.

It's a long, silent journey I take
back that night. Arriving, I brake
behind a police car at my door.
Two officers approach and, before
they speak, I guess their purpose, suggest
I'm allowed to change before my arrest.
The police cell, its pastel shades
and graffiti unpainted for decades,
confines me with my thoughts, but sleep
escapes me as a man begins to weep.
And suddenly I know it's him, caught,
caught up with, trapped, distraught,
and scratching with a coin's rim.

I call out, I question, I shout,
but the weeping and scratching continue without
abating. The night is half gone
before they stop. Moonlight that shone
through bars has slid away, lines
erased by cloud but, in the confines
of the cell and waiting to be read,
are the embezzled words of the dead.
When the lights go on and the breakfast tray
is brought by a policeman, I merely say
the night was cold, and slow, refer
to a suicide thought to occur
many years ago.

The policeman bites at my line, confirms
that a man, unable to come to terms
with his crime, hanged himself here
in the forties. I begin to peer
at the walls the moment the policeman goes,
their palimpsest of less than prose
nevertheless affecting, pain
concealed, but obvious time and again.
I find the lines I'm searching for;
words of goodbye and something more;
they're addressed to a girl whose name, engraved
on my mind, so doubly saved,
ended up in shame.

The search is over, conviction mine,
in understanding and for crime,
but one term I serve earns no parole;
I pay for the past, from which I stole,
not heredity, but a lack of will.
Not needing money or status, still
I stole, as if, in advance, in thrall
to a few lines scratched on a wall.
So when, my son, you read these lines,
mark, but don't follow, what lineage defines
and take the legitimate way. Atone
and leave the past alone.
You can live for today. They say.

Journal of a Tree

I am your post hole,
your hollowed-out log,
your slatted footpath across the bog.
I am the sapling, Greece,
spar of the western world,
I was the hull of every craft
whose sails you unfurled.

I traded with Phoenicians,
I was the Viking prow,
the galleon's mast, the dhow.
I am knowledge, the know-how
whose rings encompass the past
and what's happening now.

Christ died in my arms,
heretics perished in my fire,
for I was the crozier and the pulpit,
the rack and the pyre.

I am the Vandal's shield;
I am, and was shot from, his bow.
My forest became a battlefield,
its still-flying spear
thrown long ago.

Mine was the totem pole
of various colours and faces,
the receiver of prayers and gifts
from many creeds and races,
for I founded a log-built world
whose wooden columns recalled the old,
but I was also Cortez' wagon
laden with boxes of gold.

I am your driftwood,
your washed-up wreck,
your obsolete trencher, clogs, rebec.
I was a Saxon church,
a construct of inflammable dreams,
and I am the English heart of oak
and false Tudor beams.
I am initials carved years ago
recalling and distorting what's gone.
I am the fiddle and the bow
and the crutch old fiddlers lean on.
With me live tigers and squirrels
and multi-coloured birds
and the myriad creatures they feed on.

My charred beams on a bomb site
appear to smoulder still,
while wood pulp's piece of paper
promises peace, ignites the world
and provides the bill.

To compete with plastic,
my apparent successor
that needs no paint and doesn't decay,
what can I say?
I am simply, or simply can be,
the wonder of a burnished beech tree
you walk by one summer's day.

THE STRATAGEM

Sunlight finds the room
as though after searching.
Many summers' dust
conceals a table's sheen,
dulls a silver locket
I reach for and open. Dusk
reddens a lock of fair hair,
a history clasped
as though I'd been there.

Two centuries huddle together
    like a girl and a boy,
seem to whisper in my ear
of a secret meeting
later summers can enjoy.
Grimy Georgian windows
begin to clear, table's dust dispersing,
the lock no longer in my hand
    but outside, moonlit, dancing
    on the shoulder of a girl,
    life in every strand. The couple
    embrace; shadows of classical statues
    look on, the lock caressing
    the boy's face as the girl is held
    and kissed.
I arrive out of the darkness
    for what appears a triple tryst.

Startled, they part as I approach,
stiffen and ask where I'm from.
'Far away,' I tell them,
'where couples like you face no reproach
and the arranged marriage has largely gone.'
They wonder at my appearance
and the strange state in which I live,
each reply I give
suggesting an escape from their situation,
filial duty and dominant relation.
The girl is unsure, the boy certain
this is salvation for their fraught match;
he argues action, urges elopement.
A plan is resolved with despatch.

She cuts off a lock of her hair,
traps it in a locket with a glint of moon,
hands it to the boy. With a kiss, he leaves
to make arrangements, unaware

he's providing a rival with more room.
I beckon to the girl to follow me
into the house; we climb the steps, pass
the statues with faces of stone.

Inside, stunned, she stares at her home.
Her breath catches. What was
up-to-the-minute Sheraton furniture
is roped off, has two hundred years
of scratches. Carpets that were soft
are threadbare, faded, outdated,
walls and ceilings unfamiliar,
re-papered, re-painted.
'Where are they? – my family.
What's happened to them all?'
'They're still here, in a way.' I glance
at paintings on the wall. She slumps
on one of her newly-old chairs,
recovers a little, paces up and down.
Fingers brush artefacts no longer theirs,
her face aged by a new-born frown.
She wanders sections of a life roped off,
considers boundaries, ponders dangers.
Without warning, the doors open, admit
daylight and, more alarming to her,
a procession of strangers.

'Don't be frightened,' I reassure her.
'They're paying visitors of the National Trust.
Although they've come to inspect the past,
we can see them, but they can't see us.'
The tourists stroll, comment and stare,
approve of this, laugh at that,
admire the calm of a graceful era
and thank God they don't live there.

The girl, keen for knowledge,
also strolls, steps over the rope
to mix with the new, attempts to cope
with attitudes and conversation,
the day's newspapers a kind of guidebook
offering commentary, if not explanation.
I watch her eyes.
'They're tolerant people,' I casually say.
'Very,' she noncommittally replies;
'I should like to leave now, if I may.'

    We return to the garden and moonlight
    where statues' shadows have lengthened.
    One of them detaches itself,
    becomes the boy. He embraces her,
    his resolve to elope strengthened
    as he lists the arrangements he's made,
    enthusiasm never slowing.
    She calms him. 'I'm sorry,' she says,
    'I'm not going.'

Speechless at first, the boy remonstrates,
complains and argues for what they'd agreed,
can hardly express what his face demonstrates,
hidden doubts transformed now to need.
Before she answers, she takes his hand,
gazes at the moon and stars. The air
is fresh and clear and still.
'I was given a glimpse,' she begins,
'of our longed-for promised land.
And it might as well have been Mars.
So alien were the people, so gross,
I seem to have descended to the realm of the damned.
True, they reject our obsession with duty,
but common sense too seems to be banned,
along with the concept of beauty.
Saddened as much as horrified,
I wondered at the rate of exchange;
seeking advances, something noteworthy,
I found venality – merely change.

Love unconstrained? Elevated passion?
Their newspapers depict pornography unreined,
obscenity and violence informing fashion,
each column inch of prurience published
the gauge of a readership gained.
Must simple muslin make me a prude?
Can dignity not survive in jeans
so well as in crinoline? – or even the nude?
They swear they love, yet all their swearing
is routine, unconsidered, casual
as the clothes they're wearing
and, judging by the expressions I heard,
'sentiment' is a dirty word.
Is this the place you desire to be?
No doubt elopement would be an escape,
but does 'unconstrained' really mean 'free'?
I'm sorry, I can't go inside.
We shall never marry,
but I'll never be another's bride.'

At that, I admit I smiled.

I close the locket, mine for keeps.
Has the present
corrupted the past? Am I reviled
for securing what everyone seeks? –
for making the ephemeral last? I knew,
of course, of her conservatism
and that the boy would leave, rejection
the one thing he couldn't believe. I gaze
at the heart-shape left in dust,
then at the painting of the long-dead girl,
intelligent eyes full of trust,
hair ungreyed, skin of coral
aged by a patina easily removed.
Then, their liaison was almost immoral,
but mine too, it might be proved,
would never gain common consent.
She never married, but there's more than that.

One of the paintings, in Gainsborough's style,
depicts a child, captured, content
for all time.
His features beguile, as a child's can,
his high cheekbones and dimpled chin
something like mine. I trust his Father
was a faithful man.

Breakages

Today, we'll take tea
in elegant cups and saucers.
Biscuit? Your eyes glaze,
pale brown, remembering
how fraught was the process
that allows the chink of teatime,
civility's brittle ritual.

Fragile as porcelain, war inevitable,
designs are modified, production increased.
Fearing fragmentation, Allied
Potteries – Wedgewood, Minton,
Copeland, Spode – defend themselves
against a Dresden; contention between
Queen's Ware and Meissen.

The bomb-aimer sights
patterns on earthenware, the navigator's
map. Stoke, Fenton, Tunstall,
Burslem and Longton prepare
to be fired. But, in Hanley
a few hurried years before,
Mitchell is designing the Spitfire
that latches onto them.

Those that get through
bomb bottle kilns like skittles,
except they smash. Parian innocence
lost, flatbacks are hurled at Toby jugs
already brimming with debris. Jasperware
explodes as pieces of Willow Pattern
fly into the air like birds.
Amidst flames and smoke
and what might be charred figurines,
lie broken urns of bone china, porcelain
mixed with bone ash.

Do have another cup.
Such a beautiful day – but now,
of course, this is a smokeless zone.
You look up as an airliner
drones overhead, passengers sipping
from plastic cups, the sky a peaceful,
blue ceramic bowl.

SUBMERSION

A wave jumps
the traffic lights, still working,
green man walking
on water. A fathom below,
wipers halted mid
stride, his waxed car browses
kerbside, a shiny mollusc
with number plates.

The War Memorial
phosphoresces, bronze sailor
beyond sun's rays. A fish
slips through his fingers, darts
to the chip shop, a shoal
of battered cod in water
boiling like fat.

In the dry
cleaners, his arms wave gently,
a jacket learning to swim. Buoyed
hangers, plastic covers for lifesavers,
shoulder eddying raincoats.

Bread rises
to the bakery ceiling as a French loaf eels,
wriggled by currents. Water biscuits
dissolve by a sponge cake. Next door,
by a pond that used to reflect him,
he'd book coming summers, travel
agent's window now an aquarium.
A bikinied, cardboard girl beckons
like a mermaid, body
undulating sensuously.

Rolling to the gutter by the chemist's,
roll-on deodorants flatter drains. Flowering
tissues attract fish, lips pouting
as gloss and toothbrushes drift by.
Slimmer's biscuits settle
on the weighing machine while bubbles
from soluble aspirins aerate
the lifeboat collection box.

In his pub, every pint full, packets
of crisps, ready salted, hobnob
with wine, each bottle an occasion
that will never happen. But the morning
after, not dehydrated, has arrived.

Strange blooms wave
goodbye in the florist's underwater
breeze. A watering can hovers
over cacti and, among drowned blossoms,
a wreath wheels drunkenly, lurching,
a burial at sea, unsure
of the whereabouts of the body.

THE GRAND NITRATOR
Royal Gunpowder Mills, Waltham Abbey

Not so much a place,
more a person. Robed in calico,
no buttons or pockets,
I sat on a one-legged stool
and worked my spells.

As long ago as Crecy
I supplied the army
with firepower; centuries later
it was nitro-glycerine. Hence
the one-legged stool; I drop asleep,
I could unearth Harold II.

My black magic
blew holes in the Armada, bewitched
Guy Fawkes, the perennial firework,
sent Napoleon's Old Guard
to pastures new. I scooped out
shell holes in Flanders. Samiel an ally,
Agathe's offspring survived
the first six bullets, but not
the seven millionth. I spit black bile
which bounces in the safety tank
like Dambusters' bombs.

I worked sulphur
and saltpetre wizardry
behind feet-thick walls, mills
a touchpaper place. Bright
sparks of acolytes liked
to joke, offering fags
from a distance. Pieces of past employees,
scattered over centuries, remind
life insurance salesmen
not to call.

I am the Grand Nitrator,
destroyer of lives and homes,
master craftsman of war,
manufacturer of noise
and fragments and flames. And
I am out of work.

Now a heritage site camouflaged
by alders (charcoal) and watered
by the River Lea (transport) I am
a home for herons,
woodcocks, woodpeckers. Otters
build among reeds, as though
repairing the Möhne or Eder.
Dangerous deer,
explosions of twigs
snapping underfoot,
frighten rabbits and voles.

THE MUSEUM OF LOST ART

Are you ready
for the tour to start? Wander and gaze,
ponder the absent,
for there are no crowds, attendants
or even displays
in the Museum of Lost Art.

In the catalogue,
if we had one, this would be
our first treasure. Venus's arm.
Note the complete absence
of torso, head, legs. A non-sensual
goddess of love with vital statistics
beyond measure. Or is the sculptor making
a misogynistic comment
on sexual pleasure?

As you stroll,
hear the music we might have played.
It's probably great. Pregnant silence
wasn't the invention of Cage,
whose tantalising work echoes this piece,
blank staves potentially
first rate. Thirty years in the making,
thrill to Sibelius's symphony;
number eight.

This portrait
of Garrick captures his stage presence –
after the play. The stage is empty,
but Gainsborough has painted a cast
in one face, a multiplicity of moods,
expressions, personalities,
so that one could say, 'Here we have the man
for ever.' But incompetence
threw it away.

Sagging, dusty
and empty, our bookshelves are neon-lit,
words aglow, Alexandria's
library re-collected.
They'd all be here, the works of great minds,
the thoughts we struggle with now thought
long ago. Also those awkward books
for those with a burning desire
not to know.

On the bare stage,
left, we proudly present, if not
quite for delight, powerful drama,
ringing soliloquies,
and trust you'll find the time to experience
immortal characters illustrating
Freudian insight: Sophocles's lost plays
staged for three months.
One a night.

Now the Museum's
closing for the day. Goodnight.
At the station, you'll find other
lost arts – like manners and conversation –
on permanent display.

THE PIED PIPER

It may be simply a warning
to pay your bills. Or a folk memory
of a plague of rats, awareness dawning
that a lack of hygiene kills. Or maybe
Hamlyn had a high proportion
of get-riddable brats.

But as it was pre-pot,
pre-rave and pre-adolescence
(a recent invention) as likely as not
kids knew how to behave, smacking,
not mass-infanticide,
still being the convention.

The main madness prevailing
was cleric-led. Little's changed.
Exhorting, oppressing, religious railing
crusading for the brain-dead, Jihads
and Crusades turn a plague of rats
into a comparative blessing.

Probably a children's crusade
to the Holy Land, it truly vanished
under ground – to hell and a grave
when the wind annoyed the sand. And what
fable will Beslan become
when they've stirred the facts around?

SPQR

I wondered what it meant,
but so did the history master. He was quite good
at some things, sometimes, to some extent.

Some pupils quiver romantically.

Teaching virulence and submission, full board,
our school revered the Roman empire, tyranny
all the fees could afford.

The headmaster – a kind of Nero,
but unmusical, now burning, I trust in his
Catholic hell – took autocracy for a hero.

Sucking pleases quite rapidly.

I learned, much later, what it meant, cap
exchanged for an academic hat.
After Mussolini – hello, headmaster – claimed it,
they put it on manhole covers,
though it concealed sewage long before that.

Seeking puerile, quack remedies,
society punishes, quashing readily
students' play, Queensbury rules
cynically plied, queries rebuffed:
you'll do as we say.

Sociable penises quarrel rarely.

Sod perfection, quotas reward,
specious philosophies qualifying rationale,
so pedantic quasi-scholarship rules
sons, parents quarantining rebellion,
suspect progeny quietly rejected,
sensual pleasure questionably regarded,
sciolistic principles quintessentially
wrong.

Senatus Populus Que Romanus
shouldn't be perverted by the quixotically religious,
sophists, people with qualms about reasonableness,
scholars proposing quadrilateral rhombohedrons,
a silly poet quarrying rhymes
(I can only think of treasonableness –
not inappropriate for a betrayed boy)
struggling perpetually, questing ruefully,
surprised when portrayed a querulous renegade
whose search for personal quietude results
in stanzas, prosody, quatrains and refrains –
and if you expect sanity or an acronym,
be reasonableness; there's a limit
to these childish games.

But no end.

CONTIGUITY

Dark and early, restless, turning,
he's suddenly awake, eyes wide
at the smell of burning.
But it's only a bonfire smouldering
that tugged so hard at sleep's hem.
He looks at the clock: 4.10
    and Rome is in flames. The centuries
    strike twelve as an empire ends,
    Goths igniting the hell
    nightmare prophecy warned of so well.

He settles back into a sort of rest,
but his spirit's flame flickers and writhes,
tormented by its quest
for what? REM sleep
searches, seems to take its cue
from the time: it's 6.22.
    The Islamic era begins,
    and yet another codified tyranny
    takes a backward leap
    from peace and freedom and progress – and sleep.

Dozing fitfully again, his fears
awake, pursuing one another
like the fretful years,
he sleepwalks through an age of darkness,
senses the dragon, dawn, its harm
voiced by the seven o'clock alarm.
> Grendel stalks the night.
> Epic deeds cause epic fright
> in a world ignorant and weak,
> with little understanding of the meek.

Eventually he rises and wonders why;
to what purpose and to what end,
he enquires of the sky,
does he face each lonely day
whose empty expression tortures the time?
And the clock says, 12.29.
> The Synod of Toulouse kindles
> faith's loving Inquisition;
> you must not question this,
> unless answered by the flame's kiss.

As he ambles through the afternoon,
its heaven clear and surely free
of a lunatic moon,
he decides that art is the god
who can purge the world of ugliness swiftly.
By now it's gone 14.50
> and Hieronymus Bosch is at large,
> his overblown garden no earthly delight,
> a flowering in terror and paint
> to make the Devil himself grow faint.

He seeks escape at teatime
from oppressive, puritanical regimes;
some other clime,
if only in mind, a luxuriant
garden to generate peace and plenty.
The clock yawns: it's 16.20
    as the Pilgrim Fathers settle
    like seeds in virgin snow; life,
    new, exciting, immature,
    turns to slush and becomes impure.

He sits at home, waits for the phone
to ring, or the door, and wonders why
he's on his own;
surely the world knows
he's there and will beat a path to his door.
By now, it's gone half past four
    as Galileo recants
    Copernican views, at least in public,
    society's education
    placing itself at the centre of creation.

Although dejected, he believes he's special,
holds onto – clutches – his scripture,
his prayers, his confessional,
but the genesis of evolving doubt
seems ages ago. He queries the time
which assures him it's 18.59,
    the year of the 'Origin of Species'.
    Public opinion selects, naturally,
    the theory that suits it best,
    and God must compete like all the rest.

Time slows, though living gets faster,
hours and thoughts out of control;
both bring disaster.
He reasserts himself;
he's an individual and will not be numbered.
The clock hands lurch to 1900.
    'The Interpretation of Dreams'
    reveals the dictating, unconscious mind,
    and analysis is soon at large,
    charging for proving one's not in charge.

Stability gone, he gazes at the stars,
their light distorted by old panes,
then watches Mars
fight Newton's laws,
his whole universe determined to contrive
to alter the clock: 1905.
    Light bends, time
    contracts, fuses and confuses matter
    with energy, velocity, thought,
    which sighs for all that security taught.

He eyes the clock, stopped
at ten to three; insanity threatens.
Forced to opt
for violence, he curses the future,
and hope and each broken dream
and smashes the clock at 19.14.
    Disintegration... the death
    of love... a few poems... survival
    the enemy... madness in power...
    the eleventh, month, day, hour...

Maybe it's time for bed again.
As though he could sleep. Only uncertain
images remain,
and exhaustion, an emptiness of heart
as he ponders what's lost that seemed to be his.
Absently, he wonders what time it is…

ACKNOWLEDGEMENTS

I am grateful to the editors of the following magazines and anthologies for publication of poems, some in earlier versions.

Salzburg Festschrift: Contiguity; Journal of a Tree; Mendel, Shopping

Poets' Voice: After Dunwich

Lines Review: Journal of a Tree; Wooden Ruler; Reflected on Water

Poetry Wales: Derelict Classroom

Newbury Competition Anthology: Mendel, Shopping

Black Country Magazine: Slowing Down

New Welsh Review: Holiday Romance; Affinities; Mendel, Shopping; Lineage; Contiguity

Martello Competition Anthology: Martello Tower

Aural Images Anthology: The Figure

soundwork-uk.co.uk: After Dunwich; Derelict Classroom

Phras Competition Anthology: After Dunwich

Envoi: Contiguity; The Long Campaign

The Journal: SPQR

The Author

Neal Mason was born in Middlesex and educated in Norfolk. Many of his stories, monologues and poems have been published, and he has been successful in numerous play, story, and poetry competitions.

Neal's work was also published in *Peterloo Preview 2*, Peterloo Poets, 1990. His first poetry collection, *Excavations*, was published by Peterloo Poets in 1991. His second collection, *Leading the Guidebook Astray*, was published by University of Salzburg Press in 1995. For six months, Neal was a Writer in Residence for the Arts Council in a Welsh Valley. He tutored many courses for the University of Wales, WEA, Fairfield Arts Centre, and was awarded a bursary by the Arts Council.

Neal was selected for a five-day masterclass at Hay-on-Wye Festival and advised the Arts Council's Grants to Publishers Panel. He visited many schools, writers' groups etc. under the Writers on Tour scheme.

For the last five years, he has been running soundwork-uk.co.uk, a non-profit website that records and produces free audio plays, stories, poems, and monologues for online listeners.

Holland Park Press, founded in 2009, is a privately-owned independent company publishing literary fiction: novels, novellas, short stories; and poetry. The company is run by brother and sister team Arnold and Bernadette Jansen op de Haar, who publish an author not just a book. Holland Park Press specialises in finding new literary talent by accepting unsolicited manuscripts from authors all year round and by running competitions. It has been successful in giving older authors a chance to make their debut and in raising the profile of Dutch authors in translation.

To

Learn more about Neal Mason
Discover other interesting books
Read our blogs and news items
Find out how to submit your manuscript
Take part in one of our competitions

Visit www.hollandparkpress.co.uk

Bookshop: http://www.hollandparkpress.co.uk/books.php

Holland Park Press in the social media:

https://www.twitter.com/HollandParkPres
https://www.facebook.com/HollandParkPress
https://www.linkedin.com/company/holland-park-press
https://www.youtube.com/user/HollandParkPress
https://www.instagram.com/hollandparkpress/